Orange, Dreaming

Orange, Dreaming

K.T. Landon

Five Oaks Press
FIVE-OAKS-PRESS.COM

Copyright ©2017 K.T. Landon
All rights reserved. First print edition.

Five Oaks Press
Newburgh, NY 12550
five-oaks-press.com
editor@five-oaks-press.com

ISBN: 978-1-944355-21-0

Cover Art: Shutterstock
Cover Design: Stacey Balkun
Book Design: Stacey Balkun & Lynn Houston

Printed in the United States of America

ACKNOWLEDGMENTS

Arts & Letters PRIME: "Postlapsarian" and "An Andalusian Dog"
CALYX: A Journal of Art and Literature by Women: "The Dead Drive around Town" and "Reading Little Women in the Red Maple in My Parents' Front Yard"
Fugue: "Waning Crescent"
Ibbetson Street: "Poetry in 2120"
Jabberwock Review: "On Realizing a Friend Has Sold Me Out" and "Rise"
Muzzle: "Icebox"
Passages North: "The Dead Go Bowling"
Radar Poetry: "To My Husband, to Make Much of Time"
Soul-Lit: "On Deism Versus Theism"
Tinderbox Poetry Review: "For the Instrument"

"For the Instrument" is for Michelle Seaton

"The Dead Go Bowling" is for Laure-Anne Bosselaar

I have been so fortunate in the teachers I have worked with. Deepest gratitude to Jane Brox, Michelle Seaton, David Semanki, Laure-Anne Bosselaar, Mark Cox, Richard Jackson, Leslie Ullman, and Jamaal May, each of whom met me where I was and helped me on the road forward. I cannot repay the debt of gratitude I owe them for their wisdom, encouragement, and patience. Thanks also to poets Mary Buchinger, Edmund Jorgensen, Chloe Martin, and Adnan Onart for their friendship and for many a Saturday morning spent over these poems. Thanks to Jeanne Fraser Obbard for cover help and poetry comradeship. Thank you to Rebecca Ring, who squeezes a lifetime of friendship into one week a year. And finally, all praise to the Legendary Cow Skulls: Cynthia Dockrell, Carol Iaciofano, Kevin O'Kelly, and Julie Wittes Schlack. They know why.

For Ben, for always

CONTENTS

Postlapsarian	5
On Realizing a Friend Has Sold Me Out	6
Reading *Little Women* in the Red Maple in My Parents' Front Yard	7
An Andalusian Dog	8
The Dead Drive around Town	9
Icebox	10
The Happiness of Tomatoes in August	11
On Deism Versus Theism	12
Interstate	13
Waning Crescent	14
The Dead Go Shopping at Walmart	15
"Count Backwards Slowly from 10 to 1"	16
On Paying the Fare	17
To My Husband, to Make Much of Time	18
On My Freakish Loves	19
Poetry in 2120	20
Wild Things	21
Siren	22
The Dead Go Bowling	23
For the Instrument	24
Rise	25
Transfiguration	26

Postlapsarian

The orange dreams of the orange tree,
of heat and the low murmur of bees, of the days
when it was almost but not quite. The locket
dreams of the dark, of running silver and
unimpeded through the earth, before the hammer
and the fire. The flower dreams of the bud
dreams of the branch dreams of the seed
dreams of the flower. The mirror dreams
the sound of the ocean, dreams itself
numberless. Our bodies dream of the stars
of which we are made. They dream of
the time outside time, that last instant
of heat and light before the universe exploded,
and we shattered, and anything was possible.

On Realizing that a Friend Has Sold Me Out

Knowledge runs in one direction only.
The apple knocks Newton on the head
and suddenly—gravity exists
and a certain Aristotelian magic leaves the world
forever. The snake sells Eve on the value
of higher education and she graduates
no more naked than before but damned
if fig leaves don't suddenly seem like a good idea,
and what with God's wrath and the angel
and that flaming sword, there's no going back
to not knowing. Schrödinger says we can't know
until we look: that cat is dead and that cat
is very much alive as long as the box stays closed,
and while curiosity may or may not kill the cat,
it's the not knowing that kills us.
Ask the current Mrs. Bluebeard.
Would you go back to ignorance if you could?
Ask Simon Peter, who left his nets
by the Sea of Galilee to follow Jesus
and betray Him. Ask any of the saints
who found God but also the wheel, the rack, the stake.
There is no new thing in the world,
only we ourselves change. Understanding
clicks the facts into some suddenly
obvious arrangement. Schrödinger's cat
is dead. The scales fall from our eyes.
The garden is there: still, always.
And the sword.

Reading *Little Women* in the Red Maple in My Parents' Front Yard

Mothers of America, let your daughters
climb trees—let them risk the fall. Your girls,
for whom gravity is only a theory, are resilient.
They have not yet learned what is inevitable
and what is not. Let them be bruised, bloodied,
broken. You cannot keep them from it.
Let them claim the freedom of being unseen,
the ecstasy of perfect solitude, the stolen
green hour. Let falling be your gift to them.

An Andalusian Dog

Once is enough for Buñuel's *Chien*,
because even if you know now it was a dead calf
or a dead pig or a dead donkey,
at the time you thought it was an old, blind dog
and now the truth and the belief exist side by side,
just as your nineteen-year-old self, weeping for that dog,
still cries inside your fifty-year-old self,
pitying that foolish sophomore and, OK,
maybe never the same river twice but still,
always the same you, only more so.
Always the same little sister
in the red wool coat that matches yours,
your mother in her white uniform
laughing and talking in the tiny kitchen,
the same father home from work
with a package from the fish market that's still moving.
The days are never wholly over,
and the losses pile up but you lean into them,
you think you've learned to take it. You're fifty—
get over it—and still nineteen and still five,
and your little sister wakes up from a dream
screaming that the lobsters are in her bed,
and your mother is trying to show her there are no lobsters
and your father is yelling (your father is always yelling)
and you and your sister are both crying and you have no clue
that it will be you who tells the hospital yes,
take her corneas, and they will slice them from her eyes.
You won't be there but you can imagine it,
and though you know she won't feel it—
it wasn't the actress, after all, or even the dog—
still you cry, and you are fifty and your sister is dead,
and you are nineteen and bawling in French 103,
and you are five and there are no lobsters
and your sister is right there
beside you in the room you share,
whispering to you in the dark.

The Dead Drive Around Town

in their minivans and SUVs. We see them
in the rear-view mirror, wearing sunglasses
and smoking, even after they promised
they'd quit. They walk down the sidewalk
holding hands with strangers. At the Y
they splash in the pool with the children
we hadn't known they wanted.

The dead turn away just enough so we can't
be sure. They are busy with their other lives,
the ones their lives with us kept them from having.
They do not remember grandmother's recipe
for chicken paprikash, or who was our best friend
in fourth grade, or that time we saw Prince
in New York. They do not need us anymore.

Icebox

My refrigerator is full
of the desiccated corpses
of ginger roots, greens
dissolving into pools
of browns, sour cream
growing something
medicinal. Drawers
open to cankered citrus,
grapes half-way to raisins,
exotic fruits looking more
exotic, though less edible,
than when they arrived.
The mushrooms grow fungus
on top of fungus. Even
root vegetables are
powerless against me:
carrots swoon and potatoes
wave waxy new appendages.
Every victim of my neglect
a dream meal deferred:
boeuf bourguignon, coq
au vin, risotto, stir fry,
pasta primavera, duck
a l'orange. Every desecrated
fruit and flower and root
a dinner for two that refused
to be dinner for one.

The Happiness of Tomatoes in August

The long, slow heat. The hum
of cicadas. Green, then gold,
then scarlet: every day a new shade
of pleasure, becoming more
what they knew they were always—
every night what was bitter
turning sweet and perishable.

On Deism Versus Theism

The crane fly struggles in the dishwater—
the long legs slicked together, body
thrashing—and I cannot save her:
one more karmic failure. I should end her
suffering now, if I have a heart, but
that is not the kind of heart I have,
so I swoop down from the flies,
a *deus ex machina* for insects,
and blot her onto a paper towel,
wicking up moisture with the corners,
choosing cruelty and ridiculousness
for us both. She labors less—dying?
resting?—and I set the towel outside
in the sun. Half an hour later she is all
but free, one leg trapped in the weave
of paper. I try to ease that last delicate
limb clear, grateful that cowardice
has given me a chance at redemption
again, but in my haste I tear the leg
like the thin petal of an iris and watch
as she falls from my hand. Perhaps,
after all, the gods do not mangle us
for sport but rather from ordinary
ham-fistedness, for are we not made
in their image? Can they be other
than tired of our helplessness, of how
goddamned breakable we are? Of how
we want and want and want without
ever knowing what? They want to explain:
We're here to help, but we would not
believe them—God knows, why should we?

Interstate

The flock of starlings rises from the median like a fist,
swoops down in a single-minded dark wedge,
rises, scatters in the frozen air.

In the breakdown lane a dead Canada goose,
glossy feathers pinwheeled, shudders
in the wake of speeding metal.

The great blue heron launches himself
from beyond the guardrail,
ungainly scribble of stick legs
and flapping wings fighting for altitude,
until at last he unfolds himself, soars
across his kingdom of eight lanes.

A red-tailed hawk circles overhead,
his shadow a menace on the gray snow.

Resistance makes the power lines warm.
The doves sit in two neat lines, listening.

Waning Crescent

Children draw it
as if the better part of it
were missing but
on a clear night we see
the shadow, see what
we always see: ourselves
blotting out the sun.

The Dead Go Shopping at Walmart

for binders and embellished scrapbooks.
They wander the aisles in search of glitter
and construction paper, scissors, and glue.
They cut up their memories of us, choose
which ones to keep: the birth, the graduation,
the wedding. Ordinary days shot through
with ordinary grace. Disappointments
and unkind words, but not all of them.
They paste them onto acid-free paper,
thinking they will last forever.

The dead hold the pictures out to us.
Look, they say, grabbing our sleeves.
Remember? But all we notice are
the missing pages, the way colors
fade. We see behind the posed smiles—
or think we do, or know we can't.
We push the books aside until we can
no longer say who those people in
the old albums were. Even the dead forget.
We put them in boxes and walk away.

"Count Backwards Slowly from 10 to 1"

Blue everywhere. They move around the room,
shards in a kaleidoscope, each new configuration
a somehow inevitable surprise. The surgeon,
her wedding ring pinned to the shoulder of her scrubs.
The anesthesiologist's bifocals perched above his mask.
Beach Boys on the radio, turned low, static
from the geiger counter when it picks up dye.
No windows, stainless carts pushed against the wall,
instruments gleaming. They form a circle around the table,
run the check. *Yes*, they each say in turn. *Yes*.
The room is quiet and a flame shivers up my arm.
The nurse rubs my shoulder: *It's OK, it's OK.*
I feel their attention—cool and absolute, like truth—
and then the light of it washes over me.

On Paying the Fare

If we knew, going in, the final price,
knew the exact cost in flesh and time,
the ways we would become strangers
to ourselves—spiteful, shallow, cold—
how often we would be fools
and for how little.
If we knew how much of our longing would be
for what we ourselves destroyed,
all we would lose that might have been saved,
how many times our hearts would explode
and then gather themselves again,
knew how love would not leave us
even after it was gone,
we would, I think, pay more.
But the tracks run parallel
all the way to the horizon.
The conductor carries no cash.
We may ride no further than the destination
paid for and printed on our receipt.

To My Husband, to Make Much of Time

Is the poem about death again?
you ask and of course it's about death,
they're all about death,
every poem ever written—ever—is about
death. Lyrics? Death. Love poems? Death.
Ballads, odes, epics? Death! I guarantee you
that the man from Nantucket is deeply concerned
about his own mortality. He will die, the flowers
will fail, and the sun will burn out like someone's
forgotten cigarette. I will die, and you, my only love,
will die as well. In light of which the sensible course would be
to spend the remaining moments of our too-brief lives
in bed, with wine and maybe some pie to sustain us,
sleeping the luxurious hours between desire and desire.
But we are too American.
Except for the occasional vacation in Italy,
where they don't have good pie but make up for it
with sex in the afternoons, we turn love and fear
into work, and I am sitting in bed scribbling
as if words could save anything from anything. History
does not record whether Mr. Marvell finally got laid,
only reprints his poem again and again so that generations
of high school students can appreciate the anatomical specificity
of his vegetable love—and also the opportunity to hear
their teachers say "adore each breast" out loud in class—
but three hundred and fifty years out he still loves her fair self
and so I would you. If no one reads this except our nieces,
going through our papers when we're dead (hello, girls!),
astonished, as the young always are, to find
that they have not invented sex after all, still, know this:
what we had was made of time.
That it could not last was always the point.

On My Freakish Loves

Enthusiasm is a virtue. If I've just fallen in love
with a new song or a new poem
or a new coconut watercolor gel blush
that highlights my cheekbones with a sheer wash
of translucent color that lasts all day
you are going to hear about it. I've spent
a lifetime ashamed of my unseemly enthusiasms,
since I was 11 with frizzy red hair and braces
and blue plastic glasses, lenses smeared
with candy-coated fingerprints, raving
about some pop song that everyone else in sixth grade
had tired of months before, and I realized,
as the word "dork" entered my vocabulary,
that not only was I not pretty, but I was also
hopelessly unsophisticated, a rube
even in the hick town that is Catholic girls' school,
and that brains were not ever going to make me cool.
And though I am wiser now in the ways of taste and style,
still my impulses are suspect and I know
that the song or poem I love may reveal itself
in a week or a month to be sentimental or cheesy or just
lame. But watch the teenagers on the subway:
how exhausting to be so tired of everything, how absurd
and embarrassing the fervor of their parents'
inexplicable passions, and how much merciless work
it must have been to let go of what, as children, they adored.
Now it seems there's almost nothing left to love and,
slumped in the hard orange seats and washed-out light,
they do not look convinced it was worth it.

Poetry in 2120

In 2120, when print is obsolete and books
the province of cranks and neo-neo-Luddites, poetry
will be delivered wirelessly to your neural implant
and the poem you read (we'll still call it reading)
will finally be as good as the poem inside my head,
because it will *be* the poem inside my head
and when I write "tree" (though we may not call it
writing anymore) you will see a maple gone
incandescent in October rain, or a blue spruce
bending with snow, or some new species
that produces blossoms that smell like battery acid
and bursts into flames every 17 years and exists
nowhere, but the point is, you will see and hear every detail
exactly as I have imagined it—its height and circumference,
the veins in its leaves, the pair of mourning doves
that nests in its upper branches. And what I intend
that tree to make you feel—73% joy, 25% nostalgia,
2% regret—will be calibrated by the implant,
which will deliver the precise amount
of serotonin and dopamine required
and you will feel exactly what I feel—nothing
lost between us. In 2120, when print is obsolete
and books the province of cranks, poetry
will finally be perfect or, maybe,
it will no longer be poetry at all.

Wild Things

Kiffin knows sit and stay
only by the biscuit in my hand.
But tonight the fire engines scream past
and he howls back,
one sustained note rising at the end—
a greeting or a challenge.
The answering mayhem satisfies,
asking, at last, for something
in a language he can understand.

Siren

The sea calls us back,
longs for her missing
children, reminds us

what we are. We say
dust but the sea knows
better, tastes like blood

and tears. We long
for dissolution, fear it,
love the skin that

separates us. But the sea
beats our hearts, knows
the way to dissolve

stone. The sea tastes like
blood. Like calls to like,
and will not be denied.

The Dead Go Bowling

on Saturday nights at Starlite Lanes.
They like the way black light and neon translate
the dead and the living both into something strange
but half-remembered, a lost dialect of radiance.
They like Journey's "Separate Ways"
blasting on the sound system, the smell of Lysol,
cheap beer in plastic cups—not nostalgia, exactly,
but the way the past is superimposed on the present,
like an old camera shot where the film fails to advance,
each image occupying the other. They like the crash
of the ball and the pins, the way everything flies apart
and is swept away, only to be set up again in some new order.

For the Instrument

In the basement of the hospital
the lab tech pauses before the autoclave,
bows her head over a stainless tray,
and prays. I imagine her wearing a gold cross
or a headscarf, some emblem that could explain
love. But maybe she has pink hair and a nose ring.
Maybe she is planning to retire next spring.
Or maybe she is middle-aged and nearly invisible,
like me. She whispers over
scalpels, clamps, and retractors,
praying for their keenness and strength,
that they may be fierce in their terrible work,
that they may do no more harm
than necessary. She prays
for the surgeon and the anesthesiologist,
the nurses and residents, the patients,
the unbeliever—for me.
She closes the door, sets the timer,
attends to what's next.
This is how prayer works. Blessings,
blessings on the instrument.

Rise

The azalea speaks with the tongues
    of sparrows, shakes with the flutter
        and flick of bodies impossibly light,

bones built on air. Their voices shudder
    over and through each other, veering
        apart and then converging—many

then one—the tension between song
    and singer giving it shape, the way
        a flock rises and flies to some unseen end

and is pulled together again,
    and not one shall fall but
        the whole world trembles.

Now the brown birds rise
    and even this startled flight speaks
        of delight in feather and muscle

mastering the air—a furious beating
    of wings and hearts, an insistence
        that gravity is not the last or only law.

Transfiguration

I dreamed that I could touch the wind,
and I awoke feathered and hollow

in all my bones, and I could hold the wind,
and the wind was a living thing.

My throat opened to sing the song I knew,
but what came out was not song.

I sang the sorrow of a home lost
and the body's delight in itself.

I sang the loss of touch exchanged
for the wild pleasure of sky.

And the wind sang back to me.

www.ingramcontent.com/pod-product-compliance
Lightning Source LLC
Chambersburg PA
CBHW071759080526
44588CB00013B/2304